Lady Bird Johnson, That's Who!

The Story of a Cleaner and Greener America

Tracy Nelson Maurer

illustrated by Ginnie Hsu

HENRY HOLT AND COMPANY
NEW YORK

Henry Holt and Company, *Publishers since 1866*
Henry Holt® is a registered trademark of Macmillan Publishing Group, LLC
120 Broadway, New York, NY 10271 • mackids.com
Text copyright © 2021 by Tracy Nelson Maurer
Illustrations copyright © 2021 by Ginnie Hsu
All rights reserved.

Library of Congress Cataloging-in-Publication Data
Names: Maurer, Tracy, 1965-author. | Hsu, Ginnie, illustrator.
Title: Lady Bird Johnson, that's who! : the story of a cleaner and greener
America / Tracy Nelson Maurer ; illustrated by Ginnie Hsu.
Other titles: Story of a cleaner and greener America
Description: First edition. | New York : Henry Holt and Company, 2021.
Includes bibliographical references. | Audience: Ages 5-9 | Audience: Grades 2-3
Summary: "A lively picture book biography of Lady Bird Johnson, with a focus on her
environmentalist passion and legacy as First Lady"—Provided by publisher.
Identifiers: LCCN 2020020574 | ISBN 9781250240361 (hardcover)
Subjects: LCSH: Johnson, Lady Bird, 1912-2007—Juvenile literature. |
Environmental protection—United States—Juvenile literature. |
Urban beautification—United States—Juvenile literature. | Roadside
improvement—United States—Juvenile literature. | Presidents'
spouses—United States—Biography—Juvenile literature. | Johnson,
Lyndon B. (Lyndon Baines), 1908-1973—Juvenile literature.
Classification: LCC E848.J64 M385 2021 | DDC 973.923092 [B]—dc23
LC record available at https://lccn.loc.gov/2020020574

Our books may be purchased in bulk for promotional, educational, or business use.
Please contact your local bookseller or the Macmillan Corporate and Premium
Sales Department at (800) 221-7945 ext. 5442 or by email at
MacmillanSpecialMarkets@macmillan.com.

First edition, 2021 / Design by Liz Dresner & Sharismar Rodriguez
The illustrations for this book were created as pencil drawings and colored digitally.
Printed in China by RR Donnelley Asia Printing Solutions Ltd.,
Dongguan City, Guangdong Province.
1 3 5 7 9 10 8 6 4 2

In memory of Margaret Kathleen, a brilliant scientist
and passionate plant-lady, who believed we
can all help protect this planet
—T. N. M.

For Teresa and John Howton, Sandy, Seji, Ben, Amanda,
my Texas friends, and my family: thank you for everything, with love
—G. H.

Think small

IBM

Back in the 1950s, stinky litter and rusty junkyards lined America's highways. Billboard after billboard shouted *Buy! Buy! Buy!* Factories belched thick smoke. Garbage oozed down rivers—some rivers even caught fire!

Who would fight to make the country beautiful again?

Lady Bird Johnson,
that's who!

But Claudia Alta Taylor didn't grow up dreaming she'd be an important leader one day. "Golly, no!" she'd say. She started life in Karnack, Texas, as a lonely girl, shy as a butterfly.

Among Claudia's few playmates were the nanny's children, nicknamed Doodlebug and Stuff. They called her "Lady Bird" (another name for ladybugs). The name stuck, likely as not, because ladybugs spend their days nestled among the flowers—and so did little Lady Bird.

She especially adored the jonquils, lilies, and violets that popped open each spring. Her mother had picked wildflower bouquets, too. Mrs. Taylor died when Lady Bird was not quite six years old. Lady Bird shared her fondness for flowers.

Her father, whose work often kept him away from their country house, trusted Lady Bird to roam as she pleased. Alone, Lady Bird explored the blooming meadows, pine forests, and mysterious bayous of nearby Caddo Lake, where garlands of Spanish moss draped the old cypress trees. Her love for the wilderness grew and grew.

At age thirteen, she started her last two years of high school in nearby Marshall. The new town seemed huge to Lady Bird, with a frightening number of strangers to meet.

She slowly found friends who invited her to school football games and parties. She joined the school newspaper.

Even with her budding confidence, Lady Bird was horrified to learn she might rank at the top of her senior class. The bashful scholar would have to give a graduation speech! When the school year ended, she was one point too low to be selected for the "honor." What a relief!

At college, Lady Bird's world expanded. She studied philosophy, history, and journalism. She also acted in plays, hiding her shyness behind the characters' costumes and speaking parts.

Soon after graduation, Lady Bird met Lyndon Baines Johnson. Those two lovebirds were total opposites.

Her family came from money. His family struggled.

She preferred quiet times, reading and writing. He enjoyed socializing and talking—a lot.

She was careful and slow to make decisions. He was impulsive and always in a hurry. He even asked her to marry him on their first date!

As different as they were, they both loved nature and adventure. And they loved each other. Less than three months after they met, Lady Bird Taylor married Lyndon Baines Johnson. The couple moved to Washington, D.C., where Lyndon worked for a Texas congressman.

LBJ, as folks called her husband, won his first election to Congress in 1937. Lady Bird kept up with Lyndon's busy schedule—working with his staff, hosting dinners for policymakers, and leading city tours for important guests.

The dazzling monuments, museums, and libraries thrilled her. History! Artwork! Books! Even so, all the concrete made her homesick for her wildflowers.

Still, who stood by LBJ's side every step of the way?

Lady Bird Johnson,
that's who!

She studied political policy and learned about
campaigns. She took speech lessons. She visited
voters in Texas, enjoying long drives through the
countryside. Her confidence blossomed.

In 1943, when few women owned businesses, Lady Bird used her inheritance to buy an Austin radio station. She tended it wisely and the business grew. The Johnson family grew, too. The couple welcomed Lynda Bird in 1944 and Luci Baines in 1947. The next year LBJ won a Senate seat—with Lady Bird's support, of course.

When presidential candidate John F. Kennedy named LBJ as his vice president in 1960, Lady Bird rallied voters across the country. The team won.

Then, tragedy struck. An assassin shot and killed President Kennedy in Texas, Lady Bird's home state. Suddenly, Lady Bird's husband was president of the United States. She was thrust into the spotlight as the First Lady.

More assassinations, as well as riots, bombings, and lynchings, shattered Americans in the 1960s. Lady Bird's heart broke as her country wrestled with civil rights issues and a war in Vietnam. People seemed to see only their differences, not what they shared in common.

So, who helped to bring folks together through community projects?

Lady Bird Johnson, that's who!

She first set her sights on Washington, D.C. Lady Bird
formed the Committee for a More Beautiful Capital to
plant flowers and trees there. The group encouraged
schoolchildren to pick up litter and plant pretty gardens
in their neighborhoods, too.

Beautification spread across America.

But tackling major projects to improve and protect America's scenery—such as removing hundreds of junkyards or planting flowers and trees along thousands of miles of roadways—would take the highest levels of leadership.

Lady Bird and her staff visited political leaders, newspaper editors, and powerful businessmen to ask for support from Congress. Lobbying like this was something a First Lady was *not* expected to do.

Who delivered a powerful beautification
speech at a White House conference, as if
she'd never been shy a day in her life?

Lady Bird Johnson, that's who!

LBJ shared her concerns. He introduced a bill called the Highway Beautification Act of 1965. After late-night debates and Lady Bird's bold efforts, the law passed!

In time, native trees and wildflowers replaced litter and rusted junk along roads. Billboards came down and vistas opened. People took pride in the places where they lived.

Lady Bird Johnson didn't stop there. She worked to protect California's giant redwood trees. She drew attention to the country's polluted waterways. She helped support the Keep America Beautiful program, the Land and Water Conservation Fund, the Wild and Scenic Rivers Program, and forty-six additions to the National Park System. Over the years, she continued to champion hundreds of conservation and environmental laws and beautification projects.

Today, countless groups adopt highways and pick
up litter. Rivers run clearer than they have in decades.
And vibrant swaths of wildflowers grace roadsides
from coast to coast—Lady Bird's living legacy.

So, who fought to stop pollution?
Who helped make America cleaner
and greener?

Lady Bird Johnson,
that's who!

Claudia Alta "Lady Bird" Johnson

December 22, 1912–July 11, 2007

"Where flowers bloom, so does hope."
—LADY BIRD JOHNSON

Lady Bird Johnson and actress Helen Hayes founded the National Wildflower Research Center in Texas in 1982 as a place to study, preserve, and nurture native plants. Renamed the Lady Bird Johnson Wildflower Center in 1997, the world-famous facility at the University of Texas at Austin serves as the state's botanic garden and arboretum. It features more than nine hundred species of native Texas plants. Learn more at wildflower.org.

In 1943, Lady Bird Johnson purchased a faltering Austin radio station, KTBC, for $17,500. She added the city's first TV station in 1952. While LBJ's influence in Congress probably helped secure licenses and advertisers, Lady Bird independently ran the company. She sold the company in 2003 for $105 million.

Lady Bird Johnson successfully owned Austin's KTBC broadcasting business. She was the first wife of a president to become a millionaire on her own before her husband was elected to office.

PICK A BOUQUET OF FUN FACTS

- Lady Bird Johnson tried to ride a bicycle one time. She couldn't figure out how to stop and crashed into a mailbox. She never rode again.

- Her father gave her a car to drive herself to high school when she was just 13 years old.

- Lady Bird advocated for Head Start, the program LBJ created to help children from lower-income families prepare for kindergarten.

- No First Lady before Lady Bird had her own press secretary and a chief of staff.

- In 1964, Lady Bird traveled by train across eight Southern states to promote the Civil Rights Act and campaign for her husband—the first time a First Lady had led a solo whistle-stop tour.

- Everyone in the Johnson family used the same initials, LBJ: Lyndon Baines Johnson, Lady Bird Johnson, Lynda Bird Johnson, and Luci Baines Johnson.

Tourists flock to Washington, D.C., every year to see the clouds of pink blossoms on the city's cherry trees—some of the very same trees Lady Bird helped to plant.

BIBLIOGRAPHY

The LBJ Presidential Library in Austin, Texas, maintains an incredible collection of documents, photographs, videos, and recordings of Lady Bird Johnson and her family. Many of these are available online at lbjlibrary.org. The Library of Congress, loc.gov, also offers access to important resources. The following are some of the books I found most useful.

For Young Readers

Appelt, Kathi. *Miss Lady Bird's Wildflowers: How a First Lady Changed America.* New York: HarperCollins, 2005.

Strand, Jennifer. *Lady Bird Johnson.* Edina, MN: ABDO, 2019.

Temple, Louann Atkins. *Lady Bird Johnson: Deeds Not Words.* Indianapolis: Dog Ear, 2013.

For Adult Readers

Caroli, Betty Boyd. *Lady Bird and Lyndon: The Hidden Story of a Marriage That Made a President.* New York: Simon & Schuster, 2015.

Gillette, Michael L. *Lady Bird Johnson: An Oral History.* New York: Oxford University Press, 2012.

Johnson, Lady Bird. *A White House Diary.* New York: Holt, Rinehart and Winston, 1970.

Johnson, Lady Bird, and Carlton B. Lees. *Wildflowers Across America.* New York: Abbeville Press, 1988.

Russell, Jan Jarboe. *Lady Bird: A Biography of Mrs. Johnson.* New York: Scribner, 1999.

Video

Guggenheim, Charles, dir. *A Life: The Story of Lady Bird Johnson.* Washington, D.C.: Guggenheim Productions, 1992. DVD.

AUTHOR'S NOTE

When I was in elementary school, Mrs. LeBard and Ms. Idziorek taught us about "pollution" (a new word to us!) and challenged us to find ways to make our community cleaner and greener. We picked up roadside trash. We planted a school garden. We learned that everyone, including schoolchildren, can make a difference. I still believe that today. I hope Lady Bird Johnson's story and her bold commitment to conserving America's natural resources help inspire you to join the effort to keep America beautiful. Together, we can make our country a better place for everyone.

ACKNOWLEDGMENTS

Every book is a journey, and this has been a beautiful adventure thanks to many people: Christian Trimmer, Jessica Anderson, and the entire team at Henry Holt; Kendra Marcus and everyone at BookStop Literary; the Wordsmiths (Joyce, Michelle, Laura, and Tunie) and the Possums (Shannon, Julie, Melissa, and Ceci); the wonderfully talented Ginnie Hsu; Alexis Percle and Chris Banks at the LBJ Presidential Library; staff at the Lady Bird Johnson Wildflower Center; Anna Tong at the Lyndon B. Johnson National Historical Park; Kathi Appelt; Carolyn Crayton; my Washington Elementary teachers; and my dear friends and family, especially Mike and Tommy, who kept me going when the road took an impossibly hard turn. My heart is grateful for you all.